Smoky
the WAR dog

This paperback edition published in 2021 by New Holland Publishers
First published in 2013 by New Holland Publishers
Sydney • Auckland

Level 1, 178 Fox Valley Road, Wahroonga, NSW 2076, Australia
5/39 Woodside Ave, Northcote, Auckland 0627, New Zealand

Cover image: Australian War Memorial 026834

A catalogue record of this book is available at the British Library and at
the National Library of Australia.

ISBN: 9781760793456

Group Managing director: Fiona Schultz
Publisher: Alan Whiticker
Project editor: Kate Sherington
Designer: Kimberley Pearce
Production Director: Arlene Gippert
Printed in Australia

10 9 8 7 6 5 4 3 2 1

Keep up with New Holland Publishers:
 NewHollandPublishers
 @newhollandpublishers

Smoky
the WAR dog

**How a tiny Yorkshire Terrier became a
hero on the frontline**

NIGEL ALLSOPP

NEW
HOLLAND

DEDICATION

Naturally, I dedicate this book to Bill and Smoky, but another hero of mine also deserves a mention here – my wife, Julie. Smoky had an effect on us, too. Julie, upon our return from the holiday during which I first learned of Smoky, was diagnosed with breast cancer. Julie insisted that I pursue the Smoky story, to keep me occupied during her many chemotherapy sessions and surgeries. Thankfully, my hero is still with me.

Australian
War Animal
Memorials

PRAYER FOR AUSTRALIAN DEFENCE FORCE WAR DOGS

Gracious God and Heavenly Father, we gather to recognise one of the animals that has become known as 'man's best friend': the dog. In particular, we acknowledge the working dogs in Australia's Defence Force.

We commend to you the trainers and handlers whose love and care of their dog is absolute and who carry into battle a burden of responsibility for this canine warrior that no other soldier can experience.

With pride and gratitude, we ask your blessing on the trainers, the handlers and all Australian war dogs. Bless them and protect them, we pray, whether their service is on foreign soil or in our homeland. May they know your peace and protection as they serve in the defence of Australia.
Amen.

CONTENTS

FOREWORD

It all began so simply, in March 1944, with a four-pound Yorkshire Terrier trying to escape from a jungle foxhole in Papua New Guinea. A Yankee dog-hater, whose jeep had become stuck in the mud in the middle of nowhere, heard yapping and saw the terrier's head bobbing up out of the hole. He made the rescue and gave the dog to the motor pool sergeant, who in turn sold her to me for two Australian pounds (then around US$6.44) so that he could get back in a poker game.

Having little else to do with my spare time at Nadzab, a forward US Airbase in Papua New Guinea, I proceeded to train her in obedience and tricks. She soon became *Yank* magazine's 'Champion Mascot of the SWPA'. She went through the rest of the war with me, surviving on terrible food (not fit for dog or man), tropical heat, air raids, kamikaze attacks at sea, flying combat missions and island-hopping. Along the way, she became the first therapy dog of record.

In July 1944, when I was hospitalised with dengue fever at the US 233rd Station Hospital, my buddies brought Smoky to visit me, and she was

Smoky and Bill performing a tightrope trick.

allowed to sleep on my bed for five nights. During the day, with permission of the hospital CO (whom I learned just a few years ago was Dr Charles W. Mayo, who would become the director of the famed Mayo Clinic), Smoky accompanied the medical team on rounds, serving battlefield casualties from the Biak Island invasion. All her needs were taken care of by nurses. Then, in August 1944 when I was on leave in Australia, Smoky served the US 109th Fleet Hospital and at the 42nd General Hospital in Brisbane, escorted by Red Cross ladies. She was a huge hit doing her therapy with sick and wounded.

This continued for 10 years after the war, alongside a career in show business that saw her appear on television. She featured on one children's program that was broadcast live for 42 weeks, in which she never repeated a trick.

Strangely, following her death, it was discovered that Smoky had been born and sold to a US military couple at a veterinary hospital in Brisbane. Then called 'Christmas', her nurse owner lost her in Dobodura, New Guinea, in a crowd that was leaving a live performance of a Joe E. Brown Show.

Through the encouragement of Nigel Allsopp, one of Australia's foremost animal advocates

Bill with a Smoky memorial in Cleveland, Ohio.

and dog experts, Smoky is now being honoured by the Royal Brisbane and Women's Hospital, on an original site, where she provided support to troops 69 years ago. I am so proud that she will be remembered here, in the land of our close Second World War ally, and in the city of her birth.

Unwittingly, Smoky and I began the animal therapy movement that has proven its benefits for many of the maladies brought on during war and peace. Smoky led the way, performing her special magic, helping cure those in need, as therapy dogs are so innocently capable of doing.

My sincere thanks to the Board and staff of Royal Brisbane and Women's Hospital, and to the Australian Army Forces who participated in the ceremony honouring 'WWII's smallest soldier'.

William A. Wynne (Bill)
Mansfield, Ohio, USA, May 2013

***

The opening of the Soldier Recovery Centre at Gallipoli Barracks in Brisbane in August 2012 has been a key milestone in providing an enhanced level of care and support to wounded, injured and ill soldiers. Those returning from war with physical and mental health conditions now have a place on barracks where they can rehabilitate and recover in a safe and positive military environment.

While the centre provides dedicated staff, first class equipment and tailored programs, its use of companion dogs has been critical to its success. Harry, a Siberian Husky, was gifted to the centre by the Young Diggers Association, while Goose, a Border Collie cross, was given to an individual soldier as an assistance dog. The bonds Harry and Goose have formed with the current group of recovering soldiers are incredibly strong. I have seen Harry respond to each and every voice in the room, lie next to soldiers who are tired from a physical training session, and how his presence can entirely transform an atmosphere. Goose and his partner are also inseparable.

Anecdotal evidence suggests caring for a dog allows a soldier to focus on its needs rather than traumatic past experiences. Quite commonly, PTSD sufferers experience high anxiety in crowds, but having a dog allows the individual to socialise with the broader community and exercise or play in public areas. In Smoky's small footsteps, many therapy, companion and assistance dogs will follow. Their influence can be a potentially life-changing catalyst along a soldier's road to recovery.

It is important that the ADF continues to develop its programs and strategies to deal with complex mental health issues and care for our greatest asset: our people. Challenges undoubtedly lie ahead, but I am confident that we are prepared for the future; we will continue to work tirelessly to reduce PTSD rates, we will strive to reintegrate soldiers back into service life, and we will endeavour to provide the best possible care for those who serve our nation.

I would like to thank Nigel Allsopp for his work, and extend my deepest gratitude to the men and women of the ADF, the Young Diggers Association and the staff of the Soldier Recovery Centres across Australia. I would also like to pay tribute to service animals, past and present, who have not only enhanced the quality of countless lives, but saved them too.

Brigadier Greg Bilton
Commander 7th Brigade, June 2013

INTRODUCTION

A statue of a general on horseback rears up in just about every major city in the world, but when it comes to other military animals, dogs always seem to be forgotten. In Australia, a Yorkshire terrier no bigger than an army helmet, but with the heart of a lion, has not only been forgotten for her exploits during the Second World War, but was not acknowledged in the first place, despite her being born in Brisbane. Her name was Smoky.

In the US, the home of her owner and best friend William 'Bill' Wynne, she has been mentioned in several books, including Wynne's

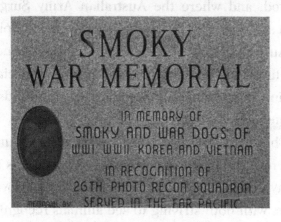

SMOKY
WAR MEMORIAL

IN MEMORY OF
SMOKY AND WAR DOGS OF
WWI WWII KOREA AND VIETNAM

IN RECOGNITION OF
26TH PHOTO RECON SQUADRON
SERVED IN THE FAR PACIFIC

An existing monument to Smoky.

own book *Yorkie Doodle Dandy* (1996), and depicted in memorials. Smoky left Australia with Wynne after the Second World War, and died in America in 1957, at the age of 14.

This book is something of a prequel to her exploits as a mascot for the United States Military, that information being well known. It's her Australian beginnings that will be explored, and her recent, final chapter in Brisbane, some 70 years after her birth.

Bill Wynne, now in his mid 90s, will at last see Smoky receive not only an Australian war dog medal, but also a permanent monument in the grounds of the Brisbane Hospital where she served, and where the Australian Army Surgical Unit still operates. Smoky will finally take her place in Australian War Dog history, as not only one of our first four-legged diggers, but also as a specialist canine who enhanced the lives of thousands of wounded Australian and American soldiers.

This is a story of two ex-servicemen, veterans of different campaigns, separated by generations and many thousands of miles, but united in their love of dogs, with both striving to see animals recognised for their contributions and sacrifices in war.

Chapter 1
The journey

My journey in this story began when I was on vacation in California. I had travelled there for a book opening at Orange County's Barnes & Noble, where my book about war dogs, *Cry Havoc*, was being promoted. Apart from having written several books on war dogs and being an ex-military dog handler, I am a war dog historian and a civilian police dog handler in Australia so, much to my wife Julie's horror, no matter where in the world I happen to be, I am always looking out for dogs who have served in this way.

On this particular occasion, we were taking a leisurely walk along Laguna Beach, when we came across a boutique pet shop. In the window was a bronze dog figurine of a Yorkshire terrier sitting in a Second World War military helmet. I just had to find out more, so I went into the shop and introduced myself. The manager pointed out that Susan Bahary, a local artist, situated in Santa Barbara, had produced the sculpture and that it depicted a dog called Smoky, a war hero. Susan is a wonderful artist, and apart from the Smoky sculpture she has produced many other war dog memorials, including her equally beautiful *Always Faithful* memorial for Second World War Dobermans killed in action in Guam.

I am a passionate advocate for the establishment of war animal memorials, so decided to contact Susan on my return home, as I thought she might be able to do some sculptures in Australia. At this time, Australia lacked much formal recognition of the deeds of war animals, in the form of plaques or statues. In fact, prior to 2012, there were no official war animal memorials on Returned Serviceman's League (RSL) ANZAC memorials in the state of Queensland, even though there have been a few private ventures around the place.

Back in Australia, I emailed Susan to compliment her on the Smoky sculpture, then basically brushed it to one side, my main aim being to see if she could produce a life-size German Shepherd for a war dog memorial I was working on. As it would turn out, I am still waiting for that German Shepherd memorial to be financed, several years down the track, while Smoky has become a big part of my life.

Fate stepped in again when Susan mentioned my interest to Bill Wynne, Smoky's Second World War handler. Bill was in his nineties, fit and well, and living in Ohio. He immediately contacted me, as he had been trying to get Smoky recognised in Australia for the best part of two decades. Smoky, he told me, was a native-born Queenslander, yet no one knew who she was or what she has done there. She'd had hundreds of articles, and some 16 books, published about her adventures in the US, along with several bronze sculptures and a medal of heroism from the People's Dispensary for Sick Animals in England, but not a word in Australian war history of her exploits.

Smoky has also featured in exhibits throughout the United States, such as the the Second World War Museum in New Orleans, and the Imperial War Museum in London, where she appeared in an exhibit on animals of war in 2010. The museum had Smoky's war blanket on display during the seven-month exhibition, representing yet another Australian connection, as the blanket was made by volunteer Australian Red Cross workers in Townsville in 1944, from the wool cover of a felt card table that Bill had purchased from a local hobby shop. Bill and Smoky had come down from New Guinea and they were cold, even in tropical Queensland, after the time they'd spent in the jungles of South-east Asia. Bill told me the US Army issued all soldiers with six woollen blankets to keep warm, but that Smoky was still shivering. Later, Smoky would wear this same designer blanket on combat missions, this time due to the cold caused by altitude, as she flew in catalinas on Air Sea Rescue missions, and again during bombing strikes on Borneo's oil fields during September through December 1944.

These stories alone would make any dog exceptional, but Smoky would go on to do so much more and help so many people during her life.

Bill's first contact with me is best recounted in his words. In his email, he told me:

A modern decorated war dog, with Sapper Shaun Ward. Photo: David Brown.

Smoky wearing her war blanket, posing with her Mascot of the Southwest Pacific War Theater of Operations trophy.

I am Bill Wynne. Susan Bahary sent me your address as Susan has done a famous sculpture of my Yorkie War Dog from WWII which has prominent place in a 22,000 acre park in Cleveland, Ohio. I was in the 5th AAF in Brisbane, Australia, Nov. '43, then in New Guinea in Dec. '43. Had two furloughs, one to Brisbane (dengue fever) and one to Sydney on combat leave. Then on through the war, ready to invade Japan from Okinawa, when the A-Bombs were dropped, ending the war. Mine is a very long story. And Smoky lives after 67 years. She has six memorials in the US, is the most famous WWII war dog of the US, appears in over 100 books ... I know of no other Aussie Publications mentioning her ... You will find in my memoir, Smoky was born in Brisbane in 1943. Took 14 years to find that out. I brought her to Australia on both furloughs and she worked in two military hospitals in Brisbane in Aug '44.

A couple of things immediately struck me after his initial email – firstly, the amazing love and passion this veteran still had for his war dog mate, nearly 70 years on, and secondly that a little Aussie four-legged digger had not been recognised for her deeds. I felt fate had brought Bill and me together somehow and that I needed to help this veteran. I do not have any grandfathers, or even a dad still living – they were all veterans themselves, of the Second World War and Korea. I would like to think that if they had a similar story and were still alive, someone would stand up and help them, so I had soon decided to champion Bill and Smoky's Aussie story.

Bill continued to send me emails about his mate, and the more I heard, the more I respected them both. Bill's aim, at his stage of his life, was to get Smoky known in her place of birth and my aim was to help him achieve this. He had already tried several Australian media outlets, to no avail, but fortunately for me, I worked with a police officer whose son, Jason Allender, owned the pet magazine *Claws and Paws*, which had many thousands of subscriptions within the State. I sent Jason Smoky's story and it took him less than a day to contact me, to say what a great story it was and that we needed to help Bill. In fact, it is important to say at this early point that everyone I have spoken to or been in contact with

For many years, soldiers and dogs have worked together in wartime. Photo: ADF Media.

has universally stated they wanted to help Bill and preserve Smoky's memory – she seems to have a magical draw or power over everyone!

Jason organised all the emails Bill had sent me into one article, and I am glad to say Smoky's story was in the magazine within a month. I was very proud to send Bill a copy. At last, one of Bill's dreams had been taken care of – formal public recognition of Smoky's Australian exploits. It only took 69 years.

My wife often says of me that I can never 'just' do something – I have to immerse myself in it until the end. Well, I guess she's right. I decided that one article was not enough for this little Aussie and his American partner, so I planned the next phase.

As the historian for the Australian Defence Force Trackers and War Dog Association, my fellow committee members and I are responsible for awarding two types of war dog medals to Australian military canines. The first is the service medal, awarded to dogs who have completed a minimum of five years service in the Australian Defence Forces or other services, such as police dogs. Due to a dog's year being roughly equivalent to seven human years, this is in effect a long service and good conduct medal, like a human would receive for 15 years of government service. The second type of medal is an operational medal. This is for Australian war dogs that have been in an operational tour of duty, such as tracker dogs that served in Vietnam, explosive detection dogs that have served in Somalia and the Solomon Islands, and currently operational dogs in Afghanistan and East Timor.

***

The Canine Service Medal (left) is issued to working dogs that have served for a continuous period of five years. The War Dog Operational Medal (right) is issued to military working dogs that have served for a minimum period of 28 days in a theatre of war, or an area of operations. Photo: Australian Defence Force Trackers and War Dog Association.

Smoky, as you will see over the following chapters, filled many military dog roles – she was a mascot, sure enough, but also a combat veteran and a medical therapy dog. The Association had never awarded a medal to a dog as far back as the Second World War, or to a dog primarily used by American servicemen. But two things helped guide us as we discussed whether Smoky was eligible for an Aussie medal. Firstly, Australian soldiers were using military working dogs as far back as the First World War. Loaned to our forces while they were serving under British command, these dogs nonetheless fought alongside Aussie troops, and were Australian war dogs in every way – even if they had to be given back to the British after the conflict. Then, during the Second World War, Allied troops supplied Australian forces with dogs to use in particular campaigns. Most notably, at the same time Smoky was working in the Pacific, and back in Australia at the Brisbane hospital, American war dogs were being used by Australian troops in the Faria Valley in New Guinea. One known example is Private J. G. Worchester of the 2/27th Australian Infantry Battalion, who was teamed with Sandy, one of the many dogs trained by the United States dog detachment for the Australian Army, to use as scouts and messengers and for forward patrols. Simply put, Sandy was a mirror image of Smoky, the Aussie dog working for the Yanks.

The second thing that was present at committee level were the members' own experiences. Three of the members had been in Vietnam, fighting as part of tracker dog teams. These men had to leave their canine team-mates in Vietnam when they came home. Due to quarantine requirements at the time, our four-legged diggers, who gave so much, asked so little and saved so many soldiers' lives, had to stay on enemy shores. The handlers did their best, finding their dogs homes with expats, diplomats and businessmen working in Vietnam, but they never got to find out what happened to them in the long run, when the Communists finally took over. This fact still haunts most of them today. I would like to relate one such story, that of Dennis Ferguson and his mate Marcus.

***

When Dennis turned 17, in late 1965, he joined the Australian Army and graduated into the Royal Australian Infantry. On graduation, he was too young for overseas service, so was told that he needed to undertake a further training course. A corporal approached him and asked if he liked dogs. When he said he did, the corporal took him to the Tracker Section, where he was allocated a dog named Marcus. Denis teamed up with another dog handler, Private Peter Hara, who has since written several great dog books and whose animal was called Caesar. The two men became good mates.

At the end of the nine months training, Denis, Marcus, Peter and Caesar were posted to the 2nd Battalion of the Royal Australian Regiment (2 RAR). After yet more training, they went off to the war in South Vietnam, with Denis, Peter and their dogs forming a part of the advance party of the Battalion in May 1967. The dogs travelled in timber kennels made especially for the trip.

On arrival at the 2 RAR lines in Nui Dat, Denis saw rows of sandbagged four-man tents, well-constructed dog kennels, and rows and rows of large rubber trees. The month between Denis and Marcus' arrival, and the arrival of the main body of the force, gave the two tracker dog teams ample opportunity to acclimatise and chase 'dummy' tracks among the rubber trees.

The patrol and tracking duties after the battalion arrived were fierce. The base was located in the province of Phouc Tuy, and the 1st Australian Task Force had the responsibility of defending the entire province. It was a big ask. Denis has said, 'While at FSPB Anderson, I took Marcus by chopper early one morning to a platoon with a 'hot' trail, and we tracked the enemy to the point where the platoon was able to complete their mission.

Then, at about midday of that day, I was picked up again by chopper and taken to another platoon, and we repeated the performance again. At about 1500hrs, Marcus and I were choppered to a third platoon, but this time the track was unsuccessful. At last light, we returned to FSPB Anderson. Three tracks in one day.'

Denis had completed thirteen months with 2 RAR at Nui Dat when his tour of duty came to an end. In June 1968, he said farewell to Marcus and handed him over to Private Alvin Peterson, without feeling too much personal emotion – Marcus still had a lot of work left in him as a military tracker dog. Denis returned to Australia aboard the *HMAS Sydney* and enjoyed ten weeks accumulated leave. He returned to duty with 2 RAR at Enoggera, but in 1969, his three-year engagement with the Army was up and he elected to be discharged.

Denis worked in various jobs for about 12 months, but found them boring and missed the camaraderie of army life. He went to the recruiting office in Brisbane and signed up for another three years. After a short familiarisation course at the Infantry Centre in Ingleburn, Denis was posted to 2nd Battalion at Lavarack Barracks in Townsville.

In May 1970, the battalion was deployed to Vietnam for its second tour of duty. On arrival at Nui Dat, a Land Rover picked Denis and his mates up, and took them to the support company lines, where he was shown his tent. It was exactly the same tent he had lived in three years previously – same bed, same chair, same table. His platoon Sergeant then took Denis to the dog kennels and said, 'That's your dog there.' Denis felt a huge wave of emotion wash over him. It was Marcus.

As Denis approached the kennels, Marcus was facing in the other direction. Years previously, Denis had used a special whistle just for Marcus, and he tried it now. The dog heard the whistle and his head went up. Denis whistled again and Marcus spun around, saw Denis and bolted for him. The dog had tears running down its face (who says dogs can't cry?) and so did Denis. There were hugs and dog licks all round, and the two mates were a tracker team again.

One incident with Marcus on his second tour involved an enemy minefield. Denis and Marcus were called to support an infantry platoon on the trail of a Viet Cong soldier, who had been seen crossing a wide-open field in full daylight.

US military working dogs work side by side with Australian troops. Many Australian dog handlers attend courses in America to learn and exchange ideas. Photo: US Army DoD Media.

The sighting was close to Nui Dat, so the team deployed by vehicle to the area where the VC had been sighted. The platoon spread out as Denis and Marcus moved to the front and the dog was cast to pick up a scent. Marcus ran from here to there and gave a multitude of alerts at the end of his three-metre tracking lead; Denis could tell from his behaviour that there was trouble at close quarter, and advised the platoon sergeant, ordering Marcus to sit while the situation was checked by radio. It was confirmed that the platoon had entered an enemy-laid minefield.

Denis carefully walked to Marcus, picked him up, and returned to safety using his own footprints in the dirt. The combat engineers from the Field Squadron arrived under the command of a captain who deployed his troops to mine-clearing work. Denis and this captain were to meet again in passing, at an Logan RSL club in 1986, where they would reminisce over a couple of beers.

The engineers cleared a large number of mines from that open field, which had been intended for use as a part of an operational deployment by A Company 2 RAR (Royal Australian Regiment) the next day. Thanks to a tracker team, many Australian lives were saved.

In 1971, Denis' tour of duty was up. Marcus was showing signs of ageing and Denis wanted the dog to return to Australia with him. He requested permission, offering to pay the $700 quarantine costs to get Marcus home, but was given a firm 'no'. The dog would stay in Vietnam. Denis was angry. He loaded a full magazine on to his rifle and approached the battalion headquarters, his anger transparent. He was ambushed by two military policemen, who apprehended and disarmed him, and immediately put him on a helicopter that flew him to *HMAS Sydney* – his ride home.

Words of farewell came from one of the police, who said: 'Son, it's all over.' But it wasn't. Having to abandon Marcus haunts Denis to this day.

***

Many dogs, including Marcus, have taken many years to get some form of recognition – but happily, in Smoky's case, the Association decided that the little terrier was indeed an Aussie war dog and that he would receive a medal.

But what medal to award?

Over the centuries, dogs have had many roles with the military. Some were official, while others were found along the way and adopted by individual soldiers. Today, military working dogs are trained for scouting, patrolling and performing building and area searches. Commanders can use the type of dog that best suits their needs, enabling the tactical commander to free up soldiers and employ their resources in other areas. While, in the past, dogs have done everything from catching rats to drawing fire to expose enemy positions, today dogs are given humane tasks, where their special skills do the most good. For many, their chief responsibilities are to warn of ambushes or attempts at infiltration.

There are many units that use dogs – for example, the engineers are often associated with explosive- and mine-detection dogs. Many countries' infantry regiments have a patrol dog capability, and special forces use dogs who are trained for both of the aforementioned roles.

Working dogs are perhaps at their most valuable when they are trained to find explosives, which they can detect in minuscule amounts across a wide range. Their assistance reduces the potential risk to persons who would otherwise have to do the search without the benefit of the dog's superior sense of smell.

Smoky was a war dog in every sense. She may not have slotted straightforwardly into one of the roles above, but she was a certified hero, a mascot, an aid to the welfare of troops, and a therapy dog at many hospitals. So, after much debate, the Association decided that the best medal for Smoky was the operational combat medal. As you will read in the following chapters, she was not an official government dog, but she had seen extensive combat and directly saved the lives of soldiers.

Chapter 2
A medal for Smoky

My big regret is that I will be unable to attend your hospital's ceremony. I am afraid the trip would be too long for me, as I am just in my nineties. That is the only thing that is holding me from coming. I would love to see Australia again and meet new friends. – Bill Wynne

On 20th July 2013, at 1430 hours, Smoky finally received some Australian recognition in the form of the Australian Defence Force Trackers and War Dog Association's War Dog Operational Medal.

The ceremony took quite a bit of planning and orchestrating, but the day went off well, with approximately 40 invited VIPs attending. Bill would have loved to have been present of course, but his age made the long trip across the Pacific impossible – a flight that, as a young man in the Second World War, he had taken many times, the last of them all the way back to the United States with Smoky smuggled aboard. He did, however, manage to be there in spirit. The week before, he prerecorded a message to all those he knew would be attending the ceremony, to thank us for the work we had done. His grandson Jon Tabar recorded him speaking at the Cleveland memorial and also in the local television station's sound studio, and sent the message to Australia for us.

In the centre of Royal Brisbane and Women's Hospital's building complex, there are several charming areas of open ground, where patients can sit and reflect. It was in one of these areas that Smoky's medal presentation took place. The hospital had set up two large plasma-screen TVs at the ceremony, so that everyone could watch Bill's pre-recorded speech. As the group gathered on the lawn of the hospital grounds, a Queensland Police Service bagpiper played a welcoming tune.

The ceremony began with the Brisbane Hospital Executive Director Dr David Alcorn opening the events, and welcoming those in attendance, who included several high-ranking military surgeons currently part of the hospital's team (and serving with the very same unit that was present at the hospital during the war, when Smoky was there). Other guests included the Patron of the police and service dogs, Dr G. Adkins, a representative of the Queensland Police Commissioner, the head of surgeons for the hospital, officers representing the Air Force and Army dog units, and handlers with their military dogs. The major VIP of the day was the US Consul General, Niels Marquardt, who had flown up from Sydney to accept the medal on behalf of Bill. The medal would be forwarded to Bill via the US Embassy in Australia.

It was, of course, not the first time Smoky had received a medal or memorial – but it was the first time in Australia. When the memorial in Cleveland Metro Park was dedicated, there were over 400 in attendance, among them military men, veterans groups, dog handlers and police with their trackers, sniffers and cadaver hunters, plus many household pets. It was a military dedication with a 21-gun salute, and a former Vietnam War medical helicopter pilot played Taps on a bugle. The local

TV weatherman sang the national anthem.

Our Australian ceremony lasted about 20 minutes, with speeches made by the hospital CEO, myself and the US Consulate General. After this, the Australian Army Padre, John Crosby, from the 2nd Combat Engineer Regiment, a unit that uses military working dogs, said a prayer, and blessed the medal and the day. Once the medal had been presented, afternoon tea was supplied, giving everyone a chance to meet each other and take some photographs for Bill.

Linda Shaw from the Yorkshire Terrier Society attended the event with a lookalike Smoky and another small Yorkie. We managed to replicate the Second World War shot of Smoky in a helmet, using a modern Australian Defence Force helmet – appropriate, I think, considering the occasion!

Another VIP that attended was a representative from the General MacArthur Museum in Brisbane. That year happened to be the 70th anniversary of the arrival of General MacArthur in Australia. Smoky and the general had much in common – they both spent time in Australia and the Pacific Islands, and on many occasions shadowed each other. Smoky was in Australia smack-bang in the

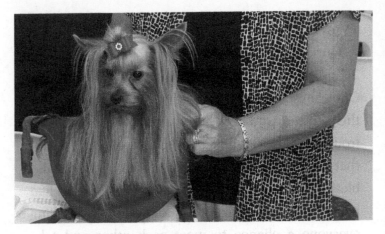

Linda Shaw and her dog Perry recreate the statue of Smoky. Photo: RBWH/Linda Shaw.

middle of General MacArthur's time in Brisbane between June 1942 and May 1944. When MacArthur moved his headquarters to Hollandia, Bill and Smoky were there for a month before moving on to Biak Island. Both landed at the same time on Luzon, remaining there until July, before moving on to Okinawa in readiness for the invasion of Japan, which was prevented by the atomic bomb and the end of the war.

The general's use of the bomb probably saved Smoky's and Bill's life. The Japanese had amassed 250,000 troops on the island of Kyushu, their next destination, and a few days before the bombs dropped, reconnaissance had showed the Japanese moving another 250,000 men onto the island. Bill told me he thinks MacArthur would have fooled them by bypassing Kyushu and bottling them up, as he did at Wewak (where 200,000 Japanese troops were present), and hitting them on a much less defended island, as the Americans needed airfields close to Tokyo. A big surprise, discovered after the war, was that the Japanese had 10,000 planes set aside for kamikaze attacks on the landing forces.

Still on Macarthur's heels, Bill's squadron went to Korea and disarmed the Japanese around Kimpo Aerodrome. Bill stated, 'As we sailed from Incheon Harbor on Nov. 1, 1945, we knew the war wasn't over, or a new one was on the horizon, as the Russians were firing at our planes if they flew over the 38th Parallel. Some ally!'

***

There is still quite a bit of guesswork involved in figuring out Smoky's exact birth date. Bill figures she was born sometime in the middle of 1943. He has some photographs, which he got from her original buyers, in which she appears to be five or six months old. That would have been before Christmas, as she was a Christmas present from Captain Heidenreich of the US Field Artillery to his fiancée, US Lieutenant Grace Guderian, an army nurse. Both were heading out on missions to New Guinea.

Bill found out that Smoky was born at the veterinary hospital and shop in Brisbane – this makes sense, as Yorkies, being so small, often have to have caesarean deliveries by veterinarians. It appears the vet was a breeder, as he issued litter registration papers to the couple, but Smoky had been the only pup in the shopfront window. The vet also stated her price – 25 Australian pounds – which meant that the average Aussie couldn't afford to purchase this pup. At war's end, Smoky's pedigree quality was quickly confirmed by a prominent breeder in the US, Goldie Stone, who wrote to Bill when Smoky's photos appeared on the front page of the *Cleveland Press* to tell him she was show stock.

Bill tends to believes that things don't 'just happen'. His friend Jim Strand, who was behind two prime memorials around the Cleveland area in the US, was a case in point.

Bill with Jim Strand (pictured right) at the
Cleveland memorial.

Bill received a phone call one day from a gruff-
voiced character. Jim had been a Vietnam Marine
medic helicopter pilot, had been shot down three
times and wounded, a hero in his own right. The call
phone went basically as follows: 'Hey Mr Wynne,
just read your book. Got a copy at the bookstore
for my wife who has a Yorkie. Smoky is a hero. I'm
going to the Metro Parks Board and tell them they
should have a memorial for her in the Park.'

And that he did.

After the memorial was approved by the council, Bill and Jim met for the first time at the park, joined by the park supervisor, to establish where and when it would be done. Bill then contacted Susan Bahary, whom he had met previously, about making a sculpture of Smoky. The park council couldn't, by law, pay for fine art, but they could do all the landscaping and design, so Jim became the driving force behind fundraising. Jim had chronic lung trouble from Agent Orange, and the world sadly lost him when he died suddenly in 2012.

There is a long string of Smoky happenings that seem to be beyond coincidence. 'The way she was lost and the way she was found was miraculous,' Bill wrote to me, 'as she wouldn't have survived in the foxhole in the heat of the New Guinea jungle, with no water, for more than a couple of hours without her discovery. Her first hospital tours for the wounded were with hospital personal volunteers from the famed Mayo Clinic, who were forward-thinking enough to allow a dog in a ward to cheer up the troops – remembering this type of medical therapy had never been seen before.

'Likewise, her work in the Brisbane hospitals, bringing about what is happening now 69 years

later through your interest and hard work Nigel ...
[I feel] fortunate to have found you through Susan
Bahary, another longtime partner in this journey.

'The discovery, at Smoky's death, as to who
lost her in New Guinea, and finding out they were
living so close to me in Parma, Ohio, all through
the years and I did not know ... She giving me the
impulse to take cover during an air attack on the
Landing Ship we were in, during the invasion of
Luzon, where buddies were wounded inches away
from me ... Even after the war my life was guided
by this little dog in the early years ...

'Right at the start, when she and I were thrust
together in New Guinea, she became my charge
and I her protector, and she would touch and be
shared by millions. It all started and progressed,
just day to ordinary day, in a tropical war ... Now
there was Nigel Allsopp, 11,000 miles away, helping
us to show her Australian place in history, which
someday may lead to a most inspirational film.

'I have always said Smoky was/is one of the very
rare and good things that happened in the Second
World War and after. She made millions happy, if
only for a few moments, just making them forget.'

Smoky's medal.
Photo: RBWH/Australian Defence Force Trackers and War
Dog Association.

Chapter 3
Four pounds of hero

Again, it is ironic that Smoky, an Aussie serving with American forces, received a hero's award from the British for work in the Pacific. War veteran Bill Wynne travelled to England to accept the award from the People's Dispensary for Sick Animals, a leading veterinary charity in the United Kingdom. Wynne was presented with a posthumous Certificate for Animal Bravery for Smoky, who was the mascot of Wynne's 26th Reconnaissance Squadron in the Pacific during the Second World War.

Early in the Luzon campaign, Smoky was called up for a task that would make her a true war dog.

Communications Sergeant Bob Gapp appeared at Bill's tent, studying Smoky seriously. He then asked Bill if he thought Smoky could pull a string through a culvert 70 feet long, eight feet in diameter.

On 12th January 1945, at Leyte Gulf, a Japanese task force had reinvaded the island by water landings, while 305 paratroops dropped on the air force headquarters of Bill's sister squadrons – the 25th Photo Recon, 20th Combat Mapping and the 3rd Emergency Rescue Squadrons (with whom Smoky had flown 12 combat missions) – in an attempt to retake the US-held airfield. Weeks later, in Luzon, US infantry divisions and combat engineers had moved forward 40 miles to Bagio, a Japanese stronghold, to retake ground and drive the Japanese from the island. If this was to be done, aircraft specialists would be needed to bolster the squadron area, and good communications were vital. It was critical that connecting phone lines be laid under the taxiway.

Sergeant Gapp explained that using Smoky would save at last three days work for a detail of men to dig up the only taxiway leading to the protected area, where P-38s , P-51 Mustang fighters and P-61 Black Widow Night Fighters were parked. If the

In Afghanistan, American and Australian troops
have adopted animals as pets, which can
relieve a great deal of combat stress. Alas,
many servicemen have to leave their pets
behind when their tour of duty is over.
Photo: American Society for the Protection of Animals.

wire-laying was done by hand digging, men would be exposed to enemy fire and all planes would have to be moved to another airfield to keep them operational, again putting both men and planes at risk. The solution was to use Smoky to crawl under the airfield's steel matting instead. The steel-matted taxiway crossed over the culvert, which allowed drainage to pass along a creek bed. Looking by flashlight, Bill could see four-inch piles of sifted sand every four inches, at overlapping corrugated steel sections. There would be just enough room for Smoky to get under. An agreement was reached with Gapp that a crew would quickly dig Smoky out if she somehow became wedged in the culvert.

When the big day came, Bill set Smoky at the far side of the pipe, ordering her to sit and stay. Gapp would feed the communication wire at the opening, checking its progress. At the far end, peering through, Bill ordered, 'Smoky, come! Come! Come on, baby!'

To Bill, it seemed to take forever. He yelled to Gapp, 'Is she still coming?'

'Yeah,' he said, 'I'm still feeding line.'

'Come on Smoke! Atta girl!' Bill urged his little pal, wherever she was.

Suddenly, about ten feet away from Bill, he saw those amber eyes glowing through the rising dust in the pipe, her long fur dancing like a show dog's. She burst out and into Bills arms, and he lifted his dog high into the air. 'Good girl! Good girl!'

Smoky had come through in about two minutes. This task kept 40 planes and 250 ground crew from being exposed to daily bombing for the three days it would have to taken to hand-dig the wires

US Marine with an English Bulldog.
Photo: US Marine Corps DoD Media.

into place. Fifty years and two generations later, there would be recognition and rewards for this little hero and, some 20 years after that, she would finally be recognised in her country of birth.

***

These days, military dogs serving alongside their human counterparts have an official military service record, which follows them through their careers. 'Official' mascots are entitled to the services of the particular army's veterinary services, as well as quartering and food at public expense. There are still also other mascots, whose costs are borne by the unit, or an individual like Bill Wynne. Mascots like Smoky have been of great moral value to soldiers, from the trenches of the First World War to the dogs adopted by Coalition forces in Afghanistan. They do not actively fight alongside soldiers, but they provide much-needed comfort to troops in adverse conditions.

Was Smoky an official mascot? She was not on the books, so to speak, and the quartermaster did not pay her bills. As Bill told me, however, everyone in his unit seemed to 'part own' her, and turning away food and treats was a full-time occupation.

What about a therapy dog? Recent headlines in US defence magazines have discussed the latest animal heroes: therapy dogs helping troops in Afghanistan. Hold the phone! The Americans can claim to be the world's first users of therapy dogs, alright, but let's remember it was done in Australia first, with an Australian dog.

***

There are still official canine mascots, such as Chesty VII of the United States Marine Corps (USMC), thanks to the German Army. During the First World War, it was rumoured that the Germans called the attacking Marines *Teufel Hunden* (as it was spelled by the Americans), translating to 'Devil Dogs', said to be a reference to the ferocious mountain dogs of Bavarian folklore. Soon afterward, a US Marine recruiting poster depicted a snarling English Bulldog wearing a Marine Corps helmet. Because of the tenacity and demeanour of the breed, the image took root. The marines soon adopted the English Bulldog as their mascot and continue to do so to this day.

The English Bulldog remains an official US Marine Corps mascot.

Photo: US Marine Corps DoD Media.

The marine base at Quantico, Virginia, obtained a registered English Bulldog, named King Bulwark. In a formal ceremony on 14 October 1922, Brigadier General Smedley D. Butler signed documents enlisting the bulldog, renamed Jiggs, for the 'term of life'. Private Jiggs then began his official duties in the US Marine Corps.

A hard-charging marine, Private Jiggs did not remain a private for long. Within three months, he was wearing corporal chevrons on his custom-made uniform. On New Year's Day, 1924, Jiggs was promoted to Sergeant, and in a meteoric rise was promoted again only seven months later, this time to Sergeant Major.

Jiggs' death on 9 January 1927 was mourned throughout the Corps. His satin-lined coffin lay in state in a hangar at Quantico, surrounded by flowers from hundreds of admirers, and he was interred with full military honours.

But a replacement was on the way. Former heavyweight boxing champion James J. 'Gene' Tunney, who had fought with the marines in France, donated his own English Bulldog. Renamed Jiggs II, he stepped into the role of his predecessor. But there was a big problem – he had no discipline!

Jiggs chased people, bit people, and showed a total lack of respect for authority. The new Jiggs would likely have made an outstanding combat marine, but barracks life did not suit him. After one of his many rampages, he died of heat exhaustion in 1928.

Nonetheless, other bulldogs followed. From the 1930s to the early 1950s, they were all named Smedley, a tribute to Gen. Butler. In the late 1950s, the marine barracks in Washington, the oldest post in the Corps, became the new home for the Corps' mascot. Renamed Chesty to honour the legendary Lieutenant General Lewis B. 'Chesty' Puller Jr., the mascot made his first formal public appearance at the evening parade on 5 July 1957. In his canine dress blues, Chesty became an immediate media darling. After the demise of the original Chesty, the replacement was named Chesty II, who was a renegade. He even escaped and went AWOL once, but two days later, he was returned in a police paddy wagon. About the only thing he ever managed to do correctly was sire a replacement.

In contrast to his father, Chesty III proved to be a model marine. He even became a favourite of neighbourhood children, for which he was awarded a good conduct medal. Other bulldogs followed (as the breed is not long-lived). When Chesty VI died after an evening parade, a marine detachment in Tennessee called Washington and reported that their local bulldog mascot, Lance Corporal Bodacious Little, was standing by for PCS orders to Washington. Upon arrival at the barracks, Lance Corporal Little was ceremoniously renamed Chesty VII. He and the English Bulldogs who followed him epitomise the fighting spirit of the US Marines. Tough, muscular, aggressive, fearless, and often arrogant, they are the ultimate canine warriors.

Modern-day therapy dogs. Like Smoky, these dogs bring joy and happiness to wounded troops.

Photos: American Humane Society.

CHAPTER 4

THE FIRST THERAPY DOG

Today, as in the past, dogs are helping service personnel rehabilitate physically and mentally after the horrors of war. In late 2001, President Bush signed a law authorising the Veterans Administration to underwrite programs like Canines for Combat Veterans, to assist in the rehabilitation of US servicemen. For many veterans, often suffering traumatic injuries, dogs give them a sense of independence they might have lost. Service dogs are 24/7 companions that can retrieve and carry objects, open doors, call attention to safety hazards, help with stress and balancing difficulties, and provide a bridge back to society. Operation Freedom, a partnership between the Veterans Administration and Freedom Service Dogs, Inc., pairs specially trained service dogs with returning military personnel and disabled veterans, to assist in the long transition from active duty and combat to civilian life.

Dogs like Smoky did assist injured servicemen with physical and mental injuries many years ago, but sadly, in earlier wars, post-traumatic stress disorder (PTSD) was often falsely attributed to cowardice, as medical staff did not understand the illness. Dogs like Smoky did not judge these veterans – they just gave them their love, if only for a short time. It is, of course, just speculation as to how many servicemen, at the Royal Brisbane and other hospitals where Smoky served, were healed by her. As we can see today, with therapy dogs, just a lick on the face or two minutes of unconditional love can help a veteran. I would like to think Smoky saved many a life.

The work Smoky pioneered has been so successful that these days another program called Paws for Purple Hearts helps US returning combat veterans by teaching those who are emotionally scarred, including soldiers with PTSD, to train dogs for their comrades with physical disabilities.

These servicemen and women first train service dogs in over 90 commands. Then, using this expert knowledge and their honed training skills, they move onto dogs that will be partnered with injured soldiers.

The process of training a service dog for a fellow veteran can help address many of the symptoms associated with psychological injuries, such as the unconditional love and support of the dogs in training, as well as stress relief, as these servicemen and women are able to reintegrate into their community. Training the dogs enhances self-worth, and provides an opportunity to practise emotional regulation, also offering a reason to participate in new social relationships. The dogs are trained to assist in the activities of daily living, by opening doors, retrieving dropped items and pulling wheelchairs. The service dog accompanies their partner everywhere – home, work, anywhere their lives take them. In many cases, they perform tasks that were previously performed by an attendant or family member, thus reducing the veteran's dependence on other people.

The Australian Army has established Soldier Recovery Centres (SRC) to support the wounded and injured. One of the ways they achieve this is by using dogs, who 'hang around' with soldiers at the centres. Many find it comforting to lie down and 'chat' with these non-judging animals, or just play with them; the dogs' workloads mainly consist of chasing balls, rolling over to be patted, and licking the odd face!

A friend of mine who suffered PTSD after his tour in Afghanistan told me he could say things to the dogs in confidence that he would never have told any human. He is doing fine now, I am glad to say, and looking forward to new challenges outside the defence force.

The first SRC was located in Townsville, Queensland, and is now operational. SRCs were rolled out in Darwin and Brisbane in early 2012. These centres provide commanders with additional resources by which to manage complex cases, members who are undertaking extended rehabilitation, and those transitioning back into a normal working life. They provide a positive recovery environment, where personnel are engaged in meaningful activities and are able to focus on their recovery mission.

The tasks all these dogs are doing are wonderful

– and, like so many things, this work has happened previously. As Bill related to me, 'Smoky began her hospital therapy work in July of 1944. I was in the US 233rd Station hospital in Nadzab New Guinea, with dengue fever. My buddies of the 26th Photo Recon Squadron came to visit and brought Smoky with them, and my mail. In the mail was a large envelope from *Yank Down Under* magazine. It was a July 14 1944 copy of the magazine and a letter congratulating me that Smoky had been chosen as the 1st Prize Best Mascot of the SWPA, owned by an individual (there was another category, for unit mascots). The *Sydney Sun* said there were over 400 entries in Smoky's individual category.

'The silver trophy would arrive much later. The trophy is now in the American Kennel Club Museum of the Dog in St Louis, Missouri, where Smoky has a display case of some of her memorabilia. There was a free one-year subscription with the prize. The July 14 issue had Smoky's photo of her sitting in a GI helmet.' This very photograph has an Australian connection, as it also featured in the *Sydney Sun* newspaper. That was the first Bill ever took of Smoky, and was the model for the Smoky bronze memorial by Susan Bahary.

The new Smoky memorial in Brisbane, based on
Susan Bahary's original. Photo: RBWH.

Bill told me that, in the hospital, two army nurses who had heard about Smoky winning the Yank contest asked if they could seek permission from their commanding officer to take Smoky on rounds. 'The wounded fellows are coming in from the Biak Island invasion and they will love her,' they told Bill. Ten minutes later, they came back to tell him they had permission and that Smoky could sleep on Bill's bed.

For the next five days and nights, until Bill was released back to his squadron, they picked Smoky up at 7am every day and brought her back at 7pm. For many years, Bill wondered what doctor had allowed Smoky to sleep with him and accompany nurses on rounds, until he happened to see a US History Channel program. It mentioned that Major/Dr Charles W. Mayo, of the world-famous Mayo Clinic, had been the commanding officer of 233rd Station Hospital in Nadzab New Guinea in 1944. The Mayo Clinic is well known for being advanced, so perhaps this is why he saw the value of Smoky's presence.

'Smoky was the first recorded dog to visit hospitals, nursing homes and orphanages, which we did for 12 years,' Bill has said. 'When I received a 15-day convalescent furlough in Coolangatta, Queensland, I took Smoky with me. I just didn't trust leaving the little dog with anyone else for such a long time.

'Stopping at the American Red Cross Riverside in Brisbane, I decided to stay there for the 15 days, after American Red Cross worker Barbara Wood Smith asked me to take Smoky to the US 109th Fleet Hospital (Navy and Marines), and then the next day to the US 42nd General Hospital, both in Brisbane. We did about 12 wards in each hospital and performed Smoky's tricks. The men followed us around to other wards and many wanted to carry her on their wheelchairs. A hospital worker suggested the hospital contact the newspaper.'

Smoky visits wounded soldiers.

Bill was worried about bringing Smoky into Australia, not knowing what the quarantine rules were, so he asked that there be no publicity. He smuggled her in his knapsack during the entire flight. Later, when he received a flying combat leave to Sydney for 10 days, he brought her back to Australia the same way.

While he was on Luzon, Barbara Smith wrote to Bill, asking if he would bring Smoky to Manila, to the 120th General Hospital. It was an 80-mile trip, but well worth it. Besides being able to serve the wounded, as the battle was still raging on Luzon and continued until the war's end, the Red Cross took photos that ran worldwide and put Bill on a live radio broadcast back to the United States. Smoky, when she arrived home in the US, became the frontpage story in the *Cleveland Press*. Four pictures were published on page one and the headline 'Yamashita to Hang for War Crimes' was shoved to the side of the page.

***

At the same time I was helping to organise Smoky's medal and memorial, I heard about a long-time interest of mine in the Australian Defence Force, in the form of a project group led by Captain Crocker and Amanda Parry, both qualified veterinarians serving in the ADF, albeit in another capacity. This project was aimed at re-establishing a Veterinary Corps within the ADF. I had previously submitted a proposal for the same thing, about five years ago, but had not heard back from anyone I wrote to.

I immediately got in contact with the ADF again and offered my services if I could in any way help the project. I noticed the new Chief of Defence (Army) had served in Mogadishu at the same time I did, and therefore would at least be aware of ADF animals, as several explosive detection dogs had been attached to 1st Battalion, Royal Australian Regiment (1 RAR) there.

The reason I broach this subject here is that in the United States and the United Kingdom, there are still existing Veterinary Corps: they look after or directly run the post-traumatic stress disorder dog teams, the very thing Smoky is most famous for in Australia, and the reason we were honouring him at the Brisbane Hospital. I made sure I also mentioned this fact at the hospital, during the medal presentation, as there were numerous high-ranking defence personnel there from the Medical Corps.

Not only do we need a veterinary service in the military here, but the work Smoky initially did all those years back could be put into practice again, with our many returning veterans from Afghanistan. The Vet Corps, if re-established, would be the ideal starting point for it. It does seem ironic that Smoky, the first therapy dog, was an Australian, yet we do not have the means to help our serving troops today with this proven and valuable method of rehabilitation.

Two Military Police working dog handlers on patrol in East Timor. Photo: Aaron Barnett.

Many of the dogs that soldiers adopt during wartime are lost souls themselves.
Photo: American Society for the Protection of Animals.

Former ADF surgeon-general and now Metro North Health Board chairman Dr Paul Alexander with the sculpture. Photo: RBWH.

CHAPTER 5
MODERN-DAY WAR DOGS

There are Smokys out there today. The 'unofficial' mascot, usually a dog, is adopted by a soldier in situ as a companion. Of all the categories of war dog, Smoky perhaps falls best into this one.

Bill had to smuggle Smoky back and forth, from his war operations in the Pacific, to Australia for his rest and recreation leave (R&R). Finally, when it came time for Bill and Smoky to go home to the United States, Bill again had to smuggle her into America. Sadly, many governments still do not appreciate the physical and mental bond between man and beast. US troops in Iraq and Afghanistan befriend local animals to help them cope with the emotional hardships they endure while deployed in a war zone, but the military bars troops from keeping pets on duty, or from taking them home, citing reasons such as health issues and difficulties in caring for the animals. Again, like Bill, some service personnel go to extreme lengths to smuggle their pets back to the US once their tour of duty is over. Many have been caught and faced disciplinary proceedings or fines.

So the Operation Baghdad Pups program stepped in, which provides veterinary care, and coordinates complicated logistics and transportation requirements, in order to reunite these beloved pets with their servicemen and women back in the US. These important animals not only help our heroes in the war zone, but also help them adjust to life back home.

Many different animals, be they dogs, cats, birds, mice or reptiles, are giving troops overseas both physical and emotional support. As with the efforts made by such organisations as the SPCA and its sister organisations throughout the world, defence chiefs must recognise these creatures as a valuable resource, not disposable assets, and allow them to return with the troops they bonded with.

Recently, the British Army was ordered to leave a dog behind in Iraq. This friendly mutt, who won the hearts of British troops, will stay on the front lines after being denied permission to live in the UK. The British government said that, after soul-searching by local commanders, 'the hero mongrel', named Sandbag, must stay in Basra.

Sandbag lived with British troops at Um Qasr until May, when Britain's mission in Iraq ended as the 20th Armoured Brigade left. Sandbag was rumoured to have been shot five times, but was credited with bringing British soldiers good luck and became a beloved mascot. More than 6,000 have signed a petition on the No. 10 Downing Street website, calling for Sandbag to receive refuge in the UK. One soldier said, 'Britain is a nation of dog lovers and this has led to many units falling for local creatures who boost morale. In Iraq, dogs are not treated well and the fear is that Sandbag will be treated badly.'

Supporters' hopes were finally dashed when the government confirmed Sandbag would stay put, saying, 'The base in Um Qasr has been handed over to American forces. Our US colleagues have

assured us that Sandbag will be well cared for.' He
was fit and healthy at the time of writing.

***

One way civilians can help military dogs in combat
zones is by sending care packages, similar to human
Red Cross parcels. The packages usually contain
some goodies for the handler, such as sweets or
biscuits, but in the main are about the dog. Items
sent might include balls, dog treats, booties and
winter coats.

In the US, the decision to send care packages
to military dogs in Afghanistan and Iraq was the
brainchild of Christopher Hamlett, a shy 13-year-
old from Mountainside whose mother, Michelle, is a
history teacher at Eastside High School in Paterson.
Christopher said he was inspired by stories his
mother told him about his grandfather, Stanley
Hamlett, who was a military policeman and dog
handler in Vietnam. 'He was so touched by these
dogs,' Michelle said. 'The thought of dogs, basically,
being trained to lose their lives broke his heart.'

Christopher wanted to get involved as part
of a social studies project. If soldiers welcomed

care packages from home, he reasoned, surely military dogs would, too. He talked to veterans and distributed about 1,000 fliers throughout Mountainside and Eastside High. The students and residents responded with donations. For the next three years, students at Eastside sent care packages to soldiers and their dogs in the Middle East.

In Australia, Jan Grew of the Gold Coast City Council organised a similar event, calling on local people to donate food or tennis balls for Australian war dogs overseas. So overwhelming was the response that a call had to be made to stop. One local tennis club alone donated 1,000 balls. In the end, with the help of the Australian Trackers and War Dog Associations Secretary John Quanne, several parcels were sent to Afghanistan and East Timor to Australian dog teams, and the rest to the Army and RAAF dog breeding facilities.

***

Smoky was an unofficial war dog on paper, but her deeds in the Second World War are being echoed today in war zones such as Iraq, where local dogs not part of any official program are being used.

An example is found in a 12-man US Special Forces unit, serving in northern Iraq, with no military working dogs of their own. They asked their Kurdish allies for a dog, and one day a scarred, underweight German Shepherd, previously used by Iraqi police, was brought to them. The Kurds had named him Tariq Aziz, after Iraq's former deputy prime minister, but Sergeant 1st Class Russell Joyce thought this an unsuitable name for a soon-to-be US K9 warrior and renamed him Fluffy.

Fluffy showed he had the heart of a lion, if not the name to match. He did not get the full military training that would normally be provided, but quickly learned to respond to commands and became a guard and pursuit dog, with Sergeant Joyce as his handler, deploying on regular assignments. He guarded Special Forces soldiers on missions, including taking control of Maqlub mountain and overcoming the last of Mosul's defences. 'He's been in harm's way and shot at more times than anyone on my team,' Joyce said.

When Joyce's unit concluded its work in Iraq, they returned to the Special Forces base at Fort Bragg, but due to quarantine laws Fluffy had to be left behind in the care of an Air Force squadron at Kirkuk. Upon Joyce's return to Fort Bragg, he frantically sent out emails asking for help. He reached numerous war dog associations and Congress members, who began lobbying for Fluffy to receive a ticket to the States. There was a tremendous outpouring of support and the red tape was cut. Approval was guaranteed, as agencies from the Department of Defence, Army, Air Force and the consultant to the Army Surgeon General for Veterinary Clinical Medicine scurried to expedite Fluffy's retirement.

When Fluffy was finally allowed to travel to the United States, it was not due to a sympathetic military, but a law established by Congress in 2000, which states that a US military working dog that is about to be euthanised at the end of his useful life may be adopted by his former handler. Fluffy was fast-tracked to the US and put up for adoption as 'military surplus'.

On 1 June 2003, Fluffy was flown from Iraq to Germany, then to Charleston Air Force Base, SC, where he was reunited with Sergeant Joyce. On 16 October 2008, K920 Fluffy, Iraq War veteran, died, having lived the last happy years of his life with his handler and owner. In war, there are few winners

Australian military working dogs today operate
wherever ADF troops are deployed, whether it's
the mountains of Afghanistan or the jungles of
East Timor.

Photo: Nigel Allsopp.

whose lives are changed wholly for the good, but Fluffy the commando dog is one of them.

Fluffy being reunited with his handler, Joyce.
Photo: US War Dogs Association.

***

As we have seen, Smoky may not have fitted into a particular category of war dog, but her exploits and duties crossed many boundaries – that of mascot, therapy dog and general war dog. There is, of course, no perfect war dog. Many a mongrel has served the colours with heroic distinction, some give the ultimate sacrifice of their lives, while others can be crippled, maimed or suffer from psychological disorders.

According to Dr Walter Burghardt, the chief of behavioural medicine for military working dog studies at Lackland Air Force Base, dogs can suffer from post-traumatic stress. Years of war and frequent deployments have affected military working dogs just as they have humans. It is amazing then that Smoky, who was exposed to the numerous sights and sounds of combat, not only got through that herself, but was able to help others along the way.

Burghardt also states, 'The dogs that go overseas are starting to show some distress-related issues. This includes hyper vigilance, or showing interest in escaping or avoiding places in which they used to be comfortable. For example, a dog that used to work at a security checkpoint or gate may try to pull away on his leash when he sees he's being led to that checkpoint or gate. Some of the dogs also become very clingy or more irritable or aggressive.

'The US Army are already treating dogs with some of these stress-related problems, but it's too early to know how prevalent it is. In the last year, about 30 cases were officially diagnosed with canine Post-Traumatic Stress Disorder. The most common behavioural problem is becoming overly active and not attentive, similar to Attention Deficit Hyperactive Disorder in humans. The average dog enters service between ages two and four, and leaves between ages eight and ten. Out of 2,000 military working dogs, 15 percent of the inventory leaves each year, and they must be evaluated for adoptability.'

***

Australians using American dogs, and an Aussie dog being used by an Americans – Smoky was just one of many such situations. The Australian Army began using patrol dogs during the Korean War, the Malayan Emergency and in Borneo. Dog training then was conducted by members of the British Army's RAVC. During the Vietnam War, the Australian Army provided two units of Tracker Dogs, but 11 of these contributors to the Australian war effort in Vietnam could not return home when their tour of duty ended. They were the six black Labradors and five cross-breed tracker dogs used by the Australian Task Force. The close attachments formed between animal and handler, and the anguish of soldiers when the time came

Sapper Shaun Ward 2CER, in Afghanistan with an ADF Explosive Detection Dog. Photo: NH.

to return to Australia at the end of their one-year tour, still emotionally affects members today.

Usually called out to follow enemy trails, or to locate suspected enemy hideouts after a contact, the teams would be airlifted by helicopter into the area of operation. The dogs loved these flights, the cool air providing a relief from the oppressive tropical heat. On the ground, the dog would be put on to the scent of retreating enemy. The dog would follow the scent, usually at speed, until a location was found, when he would stop with nose extended, facing the suspected hideout. The tracker and dog would then fall back while the rest of the section searched the area, often finding wounded enemy soldiers or recently occupied bunker systems that would otherwise have been missed.

The dogs were outstandingly successful in their combat tasks in Vietnam. Apart from their success in locating the enemy, they saved the lives of their handlers and team members on many occasions, and are credited by defence sources with saving thousands of US Army and ADF personnel lives. Sadly, many of the American military's dog teams suffered the same fate, of being left behind.

I think the best way to honour and remember these dogs is to read a poem, reproduced by kind permission of Ronald (Connie) Chronister, called *I wait by the gate*.

This same poem was read during Smoky's medal presentation at Brisbane Hospital, by John Quanne, the secretary of the Australian Defence Force Trackers and War Dog Association. When it was over, there were not many dry eyes in the crowd.

ANZAC Patrol: Military Police dog handler, Corporal David Wells, with Maximus, works with the International Stabilization Force to patrol the streets of Dili in Timor-Leste, with a section of the New Zealand Infantry.

Photo: ADF Sgt Woods.

I Wait by the Gate

In a strange land I was sent, not knowing my fate,
In a pen I was put and I sat by the gate.
I watched and I wondered, what do I do now?
Then I looked up and saw you, as you walked up and
smiled.

We trained and we worked and I showed you my best,
You rewarded me and patted me and I did the rest.
Through tracks and paths and roads we did go,
And I was to smell, for traps that would blow.

Many times I stopped you from ending your life,
From an enemy trip wire, that was set to cause strife.
Never had I thought that we would ever part,
Because of the love that we had in our hearts.

Oh, I was proud to walk by your side,
With all of your friends and being your guide.
Then one day you put me back in my pen,
You smiled, you patted me, and said, 'Goodbye my
friend.'

You looked back one more time,

And I saw the tears in your eye,

And I knew it was the last, your way of saying goodbye.

My life, it so changed when you went back home,

And I stayed behind to a fate still unknown.

It's been over 40 years since I've seen your face,

But I never forgot you, my friend and my mate.

So please don't worry, I'm waiting by heaven's gate,

For my best friend, my brother, but mainly my mate!

***

Dogs in the Australian defence force are still in great demand. In fact, there are more dogs in the ADF today than at any other time.

After Vietnam, the first Army Police Dog section was formed in 1977. The purpose of this unit was to maintain a high level of security for the Army Aviation Centre in Queensland, a role it holds to this day. It was known as the Base Support Squadron Police Dog Unit, and boasted a posted strength of five dog teams. The members were all volunteers, and came from various Corps.

The training and use of military working dogs

underwent many changes after Vietnam. Handlers were still recruited from all Corps, and retained whatever pay level they had previously been allocated. In 1990, the Military Working Dogs unit was given a singular identity, when they were incorporated into the Royal Australian Corps of Military Police (RACMP).

Today, when soldiers go to war, dogs still accompany them and form an integral part of our defence force. Australian Military Police dog handlers, attached to the International Stabilisation Force, regularly take their canine friends on ANZAC Patrols in and around the streets of suburban Dili. Military Police dogs and their handlers are a highly valued asset in peacekeeping operations.

The Royal Australian Engineers (RAE) use explosive detective dogs (EDD), who today work in a specialist search capacity to counter the threat of improvised explosive devices throughout Afghanistan within the Reconstruction Task Force. Long before the 21st century upsurge in terrorism throughout the world, military units have relied on dogs for their innate scenting abilities. This has included the safe and accurate method of detecting explosives – a fact of life in military environments.

The Army Engineers did operate a mine detection dog program as far back as 1952, when Australians operated British-trained mine detection dog during the Korean War. In 1953, the School of Military Engineering (SME) began training dogs for both guard duties and mine detection. As in several Commonwealth countries, the Australian dogs were trained using British Army doctrine. With the passage of time, the infantry took over the tracker dogs and the RAAF took over the training of guard dogs. The call for mine dogs diminished with the cessation of the Malayan Emergency, so the mine dogs section at SME was terminated in 1959. But in 1970, the Army decided to reintroduce mine- and explosive-detecting dogs in the answer to a growing combat causality lists caused by mines and improvised explosive devices (IEDs) in the Vietnam War.

The Royal Australian Navy, as a result of a fire at the Naval Air Station (NAS) NOWRA in December 1976, which completely destroyed a hangar and numerous tracker aircraft, saw the need to upgrade security, and in early 1977, police dogs were introduced to that NAS. Initially, police dogs and handlers from the RAAF were used. The first naval police and police dog teams took up duties in July 1979, with naval police dog handlers being selected from all ranks. They had to volunteer for police dog duties and at the end of the training course, the handler and his dog were posted to NAS NOWRA, where they started their new life working together. They were disbanded, however, in the 1990s.

The Royal Australian Air Force (RAAF) has utilised dogs since the Second World War. They were first introduced into the RAAF during 1943, when untrained and extremely savage dogs were placed loose inside warehouses and compounds, tied to aircraft, or fixed to long lines in such a manner that they could run back and forth. Later, patrol dogs were used by RAAF security guards to patrol the vital assets of a base.

Today, the Royal Australian Air Force is the largest single corporate user of military working dogs in Australia. Its approximately 195 dogs play an important role in the security of high-value RAAF assets, at 12 bases and establishments located across Australia. They currently have about 180 trained dog handlers on active duty.

Australian military working dogs have served

under the United Nations' flag in Sinai, Cambodia, Bougainville, Kosovo and East Timor. Current operations include explosive detection dog teams in Afghanistan and recently military police operational deployments to Timor Leste. As mentioned previously, there is still cross-Pacific cooperation between Aussie and Yankee dogs and handlers. Australian dog handlers are leading US patrols with their dogs in Afghanistan, and injured Australian dogs are treated by members of the US Army Veterinary Corps, while several RAAF dog handlers are learning instructional dog-training techniques at Lackland Air Base in Texas. Long may the bond between both peoples, as represented by Smoky, continue.

Like Bill, there has been many a dog handler who turned to his dog in the depths of war, telling him things he would never say to another soldier. Military working dogs have given a source of friendship, family and true love to their handlers in combat – the price they ask, a pat and a smile. Military canines make contributions every day. Whilst we often focus on the human cost of operations, we must never forget the ultimate sacrifices that are made by man's best friend.

In the aftermath of battle, man's best friend is
often the only mate a soldier can talk to.
Photo: US Marine Corps DoD Media.

***

Until 2000, when the law changed, US military dogs were used until they were about ten years old, then killed. It was thought that the retired dogs would not be able to adapt to family life. But decades of police and some military experience of dogs living safely on with their handlers and family members finally caused the policy to be changed.

Dog handlers had long urged that retired dogs be allowed to stay with their handlers, or be put up for adoption. The new legislation now states that the Department of Defence, in accordance with the November 2000 Robby Law, will enable military working dogs to be transferred or adopted out to former handlers, law enforcement agencies, or families who are willing and able to take on the responsibility. Currently, the Department of Defence adopts out around 300 dogs per year to private homes; of that, about 100 dogs go to law enforcement agencies outside of the Department of Defence.

Qld Governor Her Excellency Penelope Wensley AC, with VIPs, opened the Smoky statue at the Royal Brisbane Women's Hospital in December 2012.

Photo: RBWH.

Chapter 6

Smoky's legacy

The story's not over yet. After the medal ceremony, there was an overwhelming cry for a permanent sculpture at the Brisbane Hospital by many of the attending VIPs, including the hospital's own Executive Director, Dr David Alcorn. Bill himself pledged to send money over to help, and attending VIPs, such as Dr Adkins and the Commissioner of the Queensland Police Service Bob Atkinson, have offered to help pay for a bronze plaque, one of the ideas we had for commemorating Smoky. The plaque, we thought, could be attached to a sculpture of Smoky once funds were raised for it.

I am glad to add that Susan Bahary, the American artist who produced the Smoky sculpture I first saw, offered to help, alongside some other American benefactors. She kindly donated a copy of Smoky's sculpture, valued at many thousands of dollars, so that visitors will be able to see Smoky in bronze, in the grounds of the very Australian hospital in which she spent time helping US and

Smoky is finally recognised in Australia with a statue; among other humans and animals, two donkeys attended the ceremony.

Photo: Boonah Destiny.

Australian troops during the Second World War.

The ceremony was held on 12 December 2012. About a week before the sculpture arrived, the ground staff and engineers at the hospital made a special metal and sandstone memorial on which the bronze sculpture would stand, and a war animal plaque on the front. The plaque celebrates all animals who have helped troops during war – not just the operational ones, but also unofficial mascots like Smoky won the hearts of our troops and helped them get over emotional stress.

The members of the RBWH public relations and media departments worked like Trojans, organising everything from sandwiches to be served on the day to the music to be played by the piper. As the patron of the RBWH, the Queensland State Governor, Her Excellency Ms Penelope Wensley AC, was invited to unveil the statue, and kindly accepted. Once she started her speech about war animals, her sincerity was obvious, as Her Excellency is a passionate animal lover.

The handlers and animals who attended the Smoky sculpture reveal at RBWH included two members on horseback from the Queensland Police Service mounted branch, two mounted members of the 14th Mudgeeraba Light Horse Troop, dog handlers from the Queensland Police and Federal Police, a service dog from Queensland Guide Dogs and, of course, the smallest dog there, Australian Champion Karojenbe Yorkshire Terrier, Dom Perignon (Perry to us), a Smoky lookalike – in fact, he was even smaller than the original. When we put him in a Second World War helmet that we'd managed to get for photo opportunities, he could hardly see out over the top.

Representatives from the Air Force and Army Engineer dog sections were present with modern-day war dogs, some of whom were wearing their campaign medals for operations in Afghanistan and East Timor. Finally, but by no means least, were two lovely donkeys from Destiny-Boonah who, along with their owner Heike, were great crowd pleasers.

After the sculpture was formally unveiled, accompanied by speeches and poems, some 80 guests were invited to lunch at the hospital's nearby conference room. What was supposed to be a 30-minute event lasted several hours as people talked about Smoky and other war animals.

The statue is situated opposite the hospital staff's

new coffee shop and restaurant, in what is a major thoroughfare within the hospital grounds, open to the public and staff alike. Hundreds of people will see and pass Smoky every day, or be able to gaze at her memorial whilst drinking a coffee.

One thing important for the reader to know is that Smoky is still serving the hospital. A percentage of proceeds from this story will go to the Royal Brisbane Hospital, who are investigating how the money might be used to fund a new post-traumatic stress syndrome dog to walk the wards.

***

Those who stand up for our nation in time of war, putting themselves in harm's way, are heroes. We honour the men and women of the military each ANZAC Day, but there's one more group that deserves recognition: the animals that serve with people in war. Smoky, like all war animals, probably did not understand she was serving the colours just by being beside her best mate Bill. She brought a smile each day, not only to Bill's face, but to everyone she was in contact with.

Bill relayed one last story to me that, having

been in combat myself, I can understand. After a particularly hard and fierce battle one day, on one of the many islands on which they were stationed, Bill lay exhausted under cover, trying to get some much needed sleep. He awoke to hear laughter. Bill was surrounded by units of the US Marine Corps, all hardened veterans of the war. Yet the laughter was coming from these men. Bill looked up and saw Smoky jumping up in the air, trying to catch butterflies. In the depths of war and all its gruesome sights, the joy Smoky gave to those marines, for just a few minutes stayed in his and their minds forever. Smoky had worked her magic again.

Australia has lost a dozen military working dogs in Afghanistan. Sadly, on 7 June 2010, Sapper Darren Smith, his war dog Herbie and his colleague Sapper Jacob Moerland were killed by a roadside bomb. In 2012, two Special Operations military working dogs, one named Devil, were killed, alongside Sergeant Blaine Diddams. A week earlier, military dog Quake was killed whilst providing early warning for his patrol. A Special Air Service Regiment spokesperson credited the dog with having saved the lives of Australian troops on numerous occasions.

Herbie's leash is shown in the foreground, with one of his fellow war dogs. Herbie was killed in action alongside Sappers Darren Smith and Jacob Moerland; he and Darren are pictured together in the photograph.

Photo: Australian Defence Force Trackers and War Dog Association.

Memorials have been the virtues against which soldiers are measured. For distinguishing qualities, a soldier is given medals and the recognition of his country. But military working dogs also possess these qualities. Man's best friend has faithfully served the ADF in wars for many years, as scouts, sentries, messengers, and much more. They have served in many conflicts and in many cases without compensation or recognition, nor been honoured for their sacrifice. These gallant dogs have more than earned the right to be fully recognised for their service to their countries.

Sadly only a handful of all the RSLs throughout the country have stood up to honour their animal combat comrades. You, as a reader, can help in the campaign for more Australian War Animal plaques at RSLs or other suitable locations by liking the Australian War Animal Organisation, a non-profit group that helps arrange and organise these events, on Facebook.

***

In Rocky River, Ohio, the legend and legacy of Smoky continues to grow, some 70 years after her Second World War exploits. Recently, Bill got to meet a New Jersey–based Yorkshire Terrier, who is recognised in the 2010 Guinness Book of World Records as the world's smallest working dog. Like Smoky, Lucy is a therapy dog, weighing two-and-a-half pounds. Her owner, Sally Leone, trained her after she rescued Lucy from a dog shelter. When Wynne found out about the *Guinness Book*

Bill meeting Leone and Lucy, a modern Yorkie therapy dog.

achievement, he tracked Leone down and emailed her his congratulations. 'I was bowled over by his kindness,' said Leone.

A British film crew from ITV will be featuring Lucy on a show called *Super Tiny Animals*. The British wanted to know all about Lucy, but all Leone could talk about was Wynne. The TV crew saw a bigger, better story, and flew Leone and Lucy to see Bill. They met face to face in the Rocky River

Reservation of the Cleveland Metro parks, by the original memorial to Smoky.

Leone's dog was never under fire. But for more than two years now, Leone has taken Lucy to hospitals and to the homes of the ill. Lucy is good with autistic children and once lay on a man in a body cast, bringing him more cheer than he'd shown in months, Leone said. Children also read to her, as means of gaining confidence in their language skills.

***

The latest chapter in Smoky's Australian adventure began after the ceremony on 12 December, when my wife Julie said, 'We really need to go and see Bill while he is still fit and well, given he is 91 this year.' Julie needed to undergo a second mastectomy to give her the all-clear from breast cancer, both psychologically and health-wise, so my brave wife booked herself in for an operation early on in the year, to ensure enough recovery time before April, when we planned to meet Bill.

Emails flowed between Bill, Susan Bahary and Bill's children to work out a suitable time and place to meet. It was finally decided to meet at Susan's art studios in Santa Barbara, California, in early April. Bill and his son Bob Wynne flew out from Ohio a few days beforehand, while Julie and I drove up from LA, after arriving from Brisbane several days before.

Finally, after more than a year of corresponding almost daily with Bill, I got to meet him. I was surprised how overwhelmed I was; I had to take myself off to the bathroom to dry the tears from my eye. I don't know if it was the emotion of the day, the achievements we had made getting Smoky recognised, or simply because I was so glad to help this old war hero.

Susan was a great host and after lunch we sat and talked as though we were long-time friends and family. I guess I feel we are. We arranged to gather again that evening for dinner in Santa Barbara. After many hours of talking, Bill needed a rest, so we made arrangements for a final get-together in the morning. It was hard to say goodbye, even after just a few hours. Bill had made a lifetime impression on me. He is a fellow animal-lover, a hero, and is just how I hoped and imagined my grandfather, whom I never knew, might be.

I strongly believe that fate brought Bill and me together, as well as all the other people who helped us in our journey. We were meant to meet each other, and I like to think that maybe it was Smoky herself who was somehow guiding us along.

Recently returned from Afghanistan, explosive detection dog teams from 2 CER were present at Smoky's ceremonies. Photo: RBWH.

From left: Caren Caty, my wife Julie, me, Bill,
artist Susan Bahary, and Bob, Bill's son.
Photo: Nigel Allsopp.

I am a War Dog

Reproduced by kind permission Santina Lizzio

High on a hill overlooking the sea,
Stands a statue to honour and glorify me.
Me and my mates that have all gone before,
To help and protect the men of the war.

I am a war dog, I receive no pay,
With my keen, sharp senses, I show the way.
Many of us come from far and around,
Some from death row, some from the pound.

I am a member of the canine pack,
Trained for combat and life on the track.
I serve overseas in those far-off lands,
Me and my master working hand in hand.

I lift my head and look across the land,
Beside my master, I await his command.
Together we watch as we wait in the night,
If the enemy comes, we are ready to fight.

In the plantations of Nui Dat I do camp,
The smell print of the VC, to track, as I tramp.

'Seek 'em out boy!' my master does call,
Through the vines of the jungle, together we crawl.

I remember the day we were trapped underground,
With military wildfire exploding all around.
My master and I packin' death through the fight,
Comforting each other till the guns went quiet.

My master's tour of duty has come to an end,
Vietnam he will leave, I will lose a good friend.
No longer will we trudge through the jungles of war,
The canine, the digger, the memory will endure.

Now the years have passed and I patiently wait,
For God to receive me through His celestial gate.
Where I'll roam in comfort for evermore,
He'll keep me safe from the ravages of war.

About the Author

Nigel Allsopp is the Historian of the Australian Defence Force Trackers and War Dog Association, a currently serving Queensland Police Dog Handler, and well-known author, having published several books in Australia and the United States on war dogs. Nigel has been a vocal advocate for the establishment of animal memorials. Since the government announced that ANZAC history would be reintroduced into school curricula, it has been Nigel's dream to see Aussie kids taught that animals have been a big part of the ANZAC spirit.

Nigel and Bill.

Photo: Nigel Allsopp.